THE MYSTERY BOOK

Pastor Lloyd E. Stinnett D. D.

WESTBOW
PRESS®
A DIVISION OF THOMAS NELSON
& ZONDERVAN

WestBow Press books may be ordered through booksellers or by contacting:

WestBow Press
A Division of Thomas Nelson & Zondervan
1663 Liberty Drive
Bloomington, IN 47403
www.westbowpress.com
844-714-3454

ISBN: 978-1-6642-2968-6 (sc)
ISBN: 978-1-6642-2970-9 (hc)
ISBN: 978-1-6642-2969-3 (e)

Library of Congress Control Number: 2021906634

Print information available on the last page.

WestBow Press rev. date: 04/16/2021

Acknowledgements, with thanks and love to:

Jesus Christ for giving me the gift of writing.

Pastor Keith Cameron D. D.

Ollie Hayden

Rose Hayden

Arlon Benton Stinnett

Virginia L. Stinnett

Chaplain Leonard Diebold

Contents

Preface

I know I have said this to people in the past, but unless God proves me wrong, other than the children's books that I plan to write, this may be the last Christian book that I do write.

Instead of constantly putting my name on everything I write in this book, if the page does not have a different name on it, then it was something that I wrote.

Once again, let me remind you for those who do not know. The different initials I use to reference the Bible, are different versions of that scripture like N.I.V. (New International Version), or K.J.V. (King James Version). Most of the time, my usage is because it is easier to understand, and other times because I feel it explains it better.

The next page is for your personal knowledge, for you to know the difference between the four types of illnesses. Permission was given to me by: Atrium Health. You may find their site at:

AtriumHealth.org

Is it coronavirus (COVID-19), the flu, a cold or seasonal allergies?

All 4 can look very similar, making it hard to tell the difference. Use the chart below to help you decide when to seek care for your or your child's symptoms.

	Coronavirus (COVID-19)	The Flu	A Cold	Seasonal Allergies
What are the most common symptoms? Keep in mind: You may have 1 or all of those symptoms.	Fever Cough Shortness of breath or difficulty breathing Chills Repeated shaking with chills Muscle pain Headache Sore throat New loss of taste or smell	Aches Chills Cough Diarrhea (loose poop)* Fatigue Fever Headaches Runny nose Sore throat Stuffy nose Vomiting* *more common in children than adults	Cough Fever* Mucus dripping down your throat (post-nasal drip) Runny nose Sneezing Sore throat Stuffy nose Watery eyes *rare	Itchy eyes Runny nose Sneezing Stuffy nose Watery eyes
How long does it take for you to have symptoms after you are exposed?	2 to 14 days	1 to 4 days	1 to 3 days	Right away
How long do symptoms last?	Not known	3 to 7 days	7 to 10 days	As long as you're exposed to allergens

If you start to feel sick, try not to panic or think the worst.

- Coronavirus shares some of the same symptoms caused by the flu and colds, including fever and cough.
- Remember, its still cold and flu season and seasonal allergies are widespread.
- For most people who are normally healthy, coronavirus does not cause serious health problems.

How to seek care for coronavirus:

If you have a fever, cough, shortness of breath, or loss of smell and/or taste, stay home and isolate yourself from others. To find the best care, take our free COVID-19 risk assessment at AtriumHealth.org/Coronavirus, or call our 24/7 Health Line at 704-468-8888.

If your symptoms are life-threatening, call 911 immediately.

Current as of May 13, 2020

For more information, visit AtriumHealth.org/Coronavirus

 Atrium Health

Home Remedies

I am doing this section for you, to have some knowledge as to what you may do if you have allergies, a cold, and flu only. If you got COVID 19, or in severe cases of the other three, you really need to talk to a doctor or professional.

Before using any of the items listed, or any other ways to help with anything you find on the internet, in books, or advice from others, you really need to check for any side-effects, or possibly a problem with some kind of interaction that it may have to any other medication you are taking now.

Allergies

Basic kind of allergies.

Drug Allergy

Food Allergy

Insect Allergy

Latex Allergy

Mold Allergy

Pet Allergy

Pollen Allergy

There are many kinds of allergies, and also many kinds of drugs, and items you can buy that you can use to treat them.

Many people do not know this, but did you know that people used to think that tomatoes were poisonous? Why do you ask? Just as today, there are people who are allergic to them and break out.

There are over-the-counter types of pills and liquids, plus other items you can use to treat allergies, but in more severe cases you definitely need to see a physician.

The next page will give you some of the ways to help treat different types of allergies, even without using drugs. If you do some research on your own, you will find many more. If you try any of the ones listed below, you really need to take the time to do some research on the best ways to use them. If you have any side effects at all, you need to stop using any of these.

1. Saline nasal irrigation
2. Apple cider vinegar
3. HEPA filters
4. Neti pot
5. Butterbur
6. Tea
7. Bromelain
8. Spicy foods
9. Acupuncture
10. Probiotics
11. Honey
12. Humidifiers
13. Spirulina
14. Stinging nettle
15. Quercetin
16. Vitamin C
17. Peppermint essential oil
18. Frankincense essential oil
19. Herbs and supplements

Colds

These are a list of things you could try to help with colds. You will need to go on line to find out the best way to use any of these, and how they will help you. In more severe cases, you really need to go to your medical doctor.

1. Chicken soup
2. Ginger
3. Honey
4. Garlic
5. Echinacea
6. Vitamin C
7. Salt water
8. Probiotics
9. Vapor rub
10. Humidity
11. Warm baths
12. Stay hydrated
13. Rest
14. Cough drops

Flu

1. Drink plenty of fluids

2. Rest

3. Eat soup

4. Warm compress

5. Cough drops

6. Gargle with salt water

7. Neti pot

I also saw that a lot of the things mentioned for a cold will also possibly work for a flu too. Online you will also find many other possibilities that may help. My best advice for all three, whether it be allergies, the cold, or the flu lingers on, and more severe cases, you really need to see your doctor, or go to a hospital.

Foods
That
Do Not
Spoil

Fourteen food items that are said will never expire.

1. Honey
2. White and brown sugar if stored in an airtight container, away from light and heat.
3. White rice in an airtight container.
4. Salt if stored properly.
5. Cornstarch also away from light and heat, in an airtight container.
6. Distilled White Vinegar
7. Pure Vanilla Extract
8. Maple Syrup if stored properly, and you must refrigerate after opening.
9. Soy Sauce if sealed and stored in a dark place.
10. Bouillon Cubes
11. Dried Beans if stored in a cool dry place.
12. Powdered Milk if kept in a freezer till needed.
13. Popcorn left in a cool dry area.
14. Pemmican (You will need to look this one up to understand more about it.)

Demons
And
Evil
Sprits

In one of my previous books, I told you about some of the times I have encountered evil spirits. Once, when a lady friend of mine told me there was an evil spirit in her apartment which was opening and closing doors, casting items to the floor, and even one of her grandchildren was talking to someone by the furnace, even though she and others saw no-one. I and another pastor friend of mine, whose school I was going to become a minister, went over to cast whatever it was out, which we did, but that is not the end of this story. That night, even though I was new as a Christian, I blessed my apartment with oil. The next day, the pastor who went with me, said his wife was woke up in the middle of the night to check on her three little boys who slept in one king size bed. By their bed, they had a small rotating fan, that during that night fell on the bed, and got entangled in the sheets, and caught the bed on fire. Luckily enough she caught it in time, and just one of the boys got a couple of his fingers burnt. I asked my Pastor/Teacher of the ministry school, if he had blessed his apartment as I did when he got home, and he said no, but was going right home to do it then. Although that evil spirit could not come into my apartment that I blessed, we all believed it went to the Pastor's, in retribution for what we did in getting it out of that lady's apartment.

The second, which is the last one I will talk about in this book, is when I went on a cruise with a friend of mine, his wife, and his high-functioning mentally challenged son. That son was throwing up with headaches, which the family said has only happened a few times. He said he was always aware in advance that this was going to happen. As they decide to take a walk around the boat, I told them I would stay and keep an eye on him. Shortly after they left, his face got distorted and he looked at me and said in a deep voice. (This was much deeper and growly then what his normal voice was.): *"I hate you Floyd."* Next, he shook his hands like that of a referee in a ball game and said he did not mean it. Of course, I knew he did not, as he and his family have been very close friends of mine for a very long time. When his parents came back, I explained to his parents what had happened and I prayed with them, but not what I really wanted to pray, as it was a watered-down prayer not to scare their son, and let him know what I had actually thought, of him having a demon inside of him. Years later, after his step-mother passed away, and the father, son, and I went on a cruise. Although the father said it rarely happened, it happened again on that cruise, and this time I did not hold back, and put my arms around him, and prayed what I should have prayed before. Years later, the father said it has never happened again.

Both times it was the power of God, and not me. Let me make this clear. Do I ever hope that I would be put in these kinds of situations again? I hope not, as a person never knows how strong they are in the Lord Jesus, and how powerful that evil spirit may be. Let me remind you of these three scriptures of why I say this.

Matthew 17:19-21 K.J.V.: Then came the disciples to Jesus apart, and said, why could not we cast him out? And Jesus said unto them, Because of your unbelief: for verily I say unto you, if ye have faith as a grain of mustard seed, ye shall say unto this mountain, remove hence to yonder place; and it shall remove; and nothing shall be impossible unto you. Howbeit this kind goeth not out but by prayer and fasting.

Acts 19:13-16 K.J.V.: Then some of the itinerant Jewish exorcists took it upon themselves to call the name of the Lord Jesus over those who had evil spirits, saying, *"And there were seven sons of one Sceva, a Jew, and chief of the priests, which did so. exorcise you by the Jesus whom Paul preaches."* And the evil spirit answered and said, Jesus I know, and Paul I know; but who are ye? And the man in whom the evil spirit was leaped on them, and overcame them, and prevailed against them, so that they fled out of that house naked and wounded.

Matthew 12:43-45 K.J.V.: When the unclean spirit is gone out of a man, he walketh through dry places, seeking rest, and findeth none. Then he saith, I will return into my house from whence I came out; and when he is come, he findeth it empty, swept, and garnished. Then goeth he, and taketh with himself seven other spirits more wicked than himself, and they enter in and dwell there: and the last state of that man is worse than the first. Even so shall it be also unto this wicked generation.

So, with knowing these scriptures always beware, as you never know if you are prayed and fasted up enough to take them on with the power of God.

False
Gods

Before posting your next post, writing a letter, say your next word, and think your next thought, I put this section in this book because I truly care about your walk with Jesus Christ, and to let you know of some of the things that does offend Him, and He considers a sin.

I see so much of this on Facebook and other places, and it is so wrong in so many ways. First, we should never use the word Karma. The dictionary says Karma is:

(In Hinduism and Buddhism) the sum of a person's actions in this and previous states of existence, viewed as deciding their fate in future existences.

So of course, that is not from God. Also, we should never use quotes from false gods such as Buddha. The dictionary says Buddha is:

Siddhartha Gautama (also known as the Buddha *'the awakened one'*) was the leader and founder of a sect of wanderer ascetics (Sramanas), one of many sects which existed at that time all over India.

Buddha is one of the many I hear people make quotes from, and that is not right. What does the Bible say on this? This is **'God's First Commandment'**.

Exodus 20:3 K.J.V.: Thou shalt have no other gods before me.

And that would be what you are doing if you use, send out, believe any other words from any of the many false gods that are out there. Also using cards like tarot cards to tell the future, doing horoscopes, Ouija boards, occult, using psychics/mediums who say they can tell the future, are not from our God. Although there is more in the Bible talking against using these types from the devil to see the future, and even other types of practices like this, I will give you two.

Leviticus 19:31 E.S.V.: *"Do not turn to mediums or necromancers; do not seek them out, and so make yourselves unclean by them: I am the Lord your God."*

Deuteronomy 18:10-12 N.I.V.: Let no one be found among you who sacrifices their son or daughter in the fire, who practices divination or sorcery, interprets omens, engages in witchcraft, or casts spells, or who is a medium or spiritus, or who consults the dead. Anyone who does these things is detestable to the Lord; because of these same detestable practices the Lord your God will drive out those nations before you.

One last thing on this subject. I hear people always saying **'Good Luck'**, or talking about luck. Wrong! It is not luck with me. All my blessing come from our Lord Jesus Christ, in Whom I love and proudly serve. Let me give you two of many scriptures on this.

Philippians 4:19 K.J.V.: But my God shall supply all your need according to His riches in glory by Christ Jesus.

James 1:17 K.J.V.: Every good gift and every perfect gift is from above, and comes down from the Father of lights, with Whom there is no variation or shadow of turning.

Also, I am hearing people use profanity or dirty jokes which are ungodly. The worst one is using the g.d. word. I purposely did not capitalize it since I believe that is an insult to my God. Now, does God have an opinion on this? You can bet He does. I will give you just three of the many scriptures on this.

Colossians 3:8 K.J.V.: But now ye also put off all these; anger, wrath, malice, blasphemy, filthy communication (Foul language.) out of your mouth.

Ephesians 4:29 K.J.V.: Let no corrupt communication (Curse words.) proceed out of your mouth, but that which is good to the use of edifying, that it may minister grace unto the hearers.

Ephesians 5:4 N.I.V.: Nor should there be obscenity, foolish talk, or coarse joking (Dirty jokes.) which are out of place, but rather thanksgiving.

Miracles

Now that I have talked a little about how some of those nasty, wicked, evil spirits that can be in people's lives, just as much today as in the time of Jesus Christ. Although I have seen, known about, or have even been a part of many miracles in my life as a Christian in over thirty years of my life, had I done a book of all I have known about over those years, if I could even remember them all, it would have taken well over a large novel for me to write them down. Before becoming a Christian, I am not aware of any of these miraculous miracles. Although I firmly believe there are millions a day happening. I am just going to tell you of four from the first one I remember when first being saved, to three others that had affected me personally.

I

When first becoming a Christian, I lived in a very small town called Elm Springs Arkansas, right out of Springdale Arkansas. There was a small country church of maybe 30 members that attended there. This is the church where I actually got saved, and turned my life over to Jesus Christ.

Although I was newly saved, I truly did not understand the true power of a living God. Knowing this, there was an eleven-year-old boy who had cancer about the size of a hardball right next to his heart. It would have been a very delicate and risky operation. Although he did not go to this church, the church I was going to, and eight others were praying for him. Of course, being new to this praying for others process, I gave it my very best. The day of the operation the doctors felt it would be good to take more pictures, in order to help them in a possibly deadly operation. To their surprise it was gone. In their disbelief they decided to cut a very small incision, and somehow be able to possibly see what the pictures may have missed. Needless to say, they did not need to do that operation. This is the first miracle that I have ever known in my lifetime. Even though I still did not understand God's power and how He worked, this increased my faith in Him.

II

Even though I have seen and heard of many more miracles happening since my rebirth, in my life with Jesus Christ, let me fast forward you to when I moved to Nashville Tennessee a few years later. Not sure, but this happened a few months after I started to ministry school, close to where I lived. A friend of mine, who also lived in the apartment complex, invited me to her brother's church. Truthfully, I probably learned more from going to that church then I did in the school I went to for about a year, to get my minister's license. Shortly after going there, the pastor and I became very good friends, and he took me under his wing so to speak. He gave me all the opportunities a person would need to go into the ministry. Teaching on Wednesday nights, as he was bi-vocational and had to work some of those nights, sing solos, collect tithes and offerings, a greeter, teach the adult class, and of course the little children's class.

Generally, when I sing a solo, I like to practice it a lot before doing it in public. At this time, I had been going to the church I talked about for over six-eight months with a congregation of about thirty-five people. I found a song I felt led to do called **'The Altar'**. After only practicing it a couple times, I told the pastor of that church that I felt led to do this song for the altar call and he agreed. The lyrics were written on a very small card, and being a song I was not very familiar with, I stayed focused on that card. When through, I looked over the pulpit and saw the pews empty, and only one person sitting in them. A man whose wife participated a lot in that church, but he usually just came when they had dinners, which they were doing that day. After walking away from the pulpit, I noticed everyone else at the altar crying and hugging each other. Although I was doing all that I was doing in that church that I talked about in the previous paragraph, I was unaware that half the church were in conflict with the other half of the church, for what ever reason I am still not aware of. It was the power of God and not me, and He used that song, that day, for all of them to make amends, and for that church to once again come into unity.

III

Now to a more serious healing that I had, which when it happened, I was extremely scared about it.

Many years ago, I went to my doctor who was a General Practitioner. She put the stethoscope to my heart, and then she looked very worried. She left and came back in with a strange looking machine, that I guess that monitored my heart and ran the results on a skinny piece of paper. She advised me to see a heart specialist very soon. From then on, I became very scared of what I would find out.

I could not get an appointment for a couple weeks, Needless to say, I could not get the thoughts of what I would find out, out of my mind. I remembered about the boy with cancer by his heart that I first talked about. So, I asked people in churches in five different states that my ministry was connected with to pray for me, and many in and around the Nashville area. I even called every 800 number I could find that had a prayer line to pray for me.

I am not sure if this has happened to you or not, but sometimes I feel the Holy Spirit move within me. Some people say it feels like goose bumps, or a tingling sensation. At least a couple times I felt the Holy Spirit move throughout my body, but most of the time it starts at my left leg for some reason.

Now saying that, this was quite different. Two nights before seeing the heart specialist, I was awakened in the middle of the night twice, both times with that tingling sensation only around my heart, about the size of a dinner plate. The next night the same thing happened, but only once. I went to the heart doctor, and he ran a bunch of tests, and said everything was fine. I had a strange look on my face, so he said he could run more tests if I would like. At that time, I knew, that I did have a major heart problem, and God did heal me. **'Praise the Lord.'** I guess He had much more for me to do. Actually, this happened again a few years later. I did not see a doctor then, since I realized that there must have been a problem with my heart again, and that God once again, did a miraculous healing in me. I was convinced then as I do now, that God was not through with me in what He wants me to do here on earth.

A funny thing about this story, when people asked me how it went. I told them that the doctor said my heart was strong as an ox, and I was twice as smart. L.O.L. Well the first part was true anyway.

IV

As I could go on and on about the miracles, I have seen, heard or know about, I think I will quit at this one. This too, makes me think that God is not through with me in serving Him. What I am about to tell you is either an almost impossible coincidence, or the devil was trying to take me out, and God overrode him all three times.

Over the last couple years, I had to go to the emergency room, and two times stayed in the hospital for a few days. Each time oddly enough, I was doing something major in one of my five books that told the truth about the devil and his ungodly followers. One time I was in the hospital for about six days, another four days, and the last just in the emergency room for about ten hours. Each time, besides what I went to the hospital for, my blood pressure was over 200. Any of those times I could have had a heart attack, or a stroke. Needless to say, it did not happen any of those times. Was this an attack on me from Satan. I firmly believe it was. Had it been one of the books, maybe even two in which it happened, it may have possibly be happenstance, but not three, especially when I was attacking Satan and his devilish evil imps, and letting people know the truth about him, and how truly evil he and his ungodly followers are, and how they are trying to get as many people as possible to go to hell with them for eternity. This is something you all really need to think about, if you are one of those who are still denying Jesus Christ to come into your life.

Before going to the section called **'Modern Day Psalms'**, I would like to give you two of my very favorite, and powerful Psalm scriptures in the Bible. My third favorite is Psalm 119, which is quite lengthy, and I will let you look that one up that for yourself.

23rd Psalm K.J.V.

The Lord is my shepherd; I shall not want. He maketh me to lie down in green pastures: He leadeth me beside the still waters. He restoreth my soul: He leadeth me in the paths of righteousness for His Name's Sake. Yea, though I walk through the valley of the shadow of death, I will fear no evil: for Thou art with me; Thy rod and Thy staff they comfort me. Thou preparest a table before me in the presence of mine enemies: Thou anointest my head with oil; my cup runneth over. Surely goodness and mercy shall follow me all the days of my life: and I will dwell in the house of the Lord forever.

91st Psalm K.J.V.

He that dwelleth in the secret place of the most High shall abide under the shadow of the Almighty. I will say of the Lord, He is my refuge and my fortress: my God; in Him will I trust. Surely, He shall deliver thee from the snare of the fowler, and from the noisome pestilence. He shall cover thee with His feathers, and under His wings shalt thou trust: His truth shall be thy shield and buckler. Thou shalt not be afraid for the terror by night; nor for the arrow that flieth by day; Nor for the pestilence that walketh in darkness; nor for the destruction that wasteth at noonday. A thousand shall fall at thy side, and ten thousand at thy right hand; but it shall not come nigh thee. Only with thine eyes shalt thou behold and see the reward of the wicked. Because thou hast made the Lord, which is my refuge, even the most High, thy habitation; There shall no evil befall thee, neither shall any plague come nigh thy dwelling. For He shall give His angels charge over thee, to keep thee in all Thy ways. They shall bear thee up in their hands, lest thou dash thy foot against a stone. Thou shalt tread upon the lion and adder: the young lion and the dragon shalt thou trample under feet. Because

He hath set his love upon Me, therefore will I deliver him: I will set him on high, because he hath known My name. He shall call upon Me, and I will answer him: I will be with him in trouble; I will deliver him, and honor him. With long life will I satisfy him, and shew him My salvation.

Modern
Day
Psalms

Please remember, although I felt led that this should be the title of this section, I am not putting it on the same caliber of the Psalms in the Bible.

I

Lord, sometimes my mind regresses to the past,
of the thoughts I had as a small child.
Innocent and naive to one
who later became evil and wicked.
These later thoughts sometimes clutter my mind
with sadness, grief, and regrets.
I realize that the man I am now is truly different,
than the one which laid down so many sins,
against ever so many people before Thee.
I cannot change any of that,
as I do not have the power to change my past,
if I ever could.
Now I try to live a better life serving You,
with the few remaining years, I have left here on earth.
With the life I set upon myself,
from my past transgressions,
at time I feel the loneliness,
a void, and emptiness.
I do not do what I do,
in thoughts that it would erase or compensate
in any way for the past life that I had led.
To even think of the forgiveness,
You would have to give me over whelms my mind.

My love for You is strong.
Now, I can only hope and pray,
that for all those I have wronged,
that they can find the compassion in
their hearts to forgive me,
and find their eternal salvation
in Jesus Christ.

II

Dear Lord,
please forgive me as I feel so lost and bewildered,
in all of my flawed attempts,
to reach those who are lost and back slidden.
They are so taken in
by what this evil and wicked world has to offer,
that so many do not want to heed
to Thy word.
Almost daily I feel as if I have failed You
in my actions and deeds.
Please find Your favor in me,
and please forgive me whenever
I have wronged You.

III

To The Great I Am.

To the Great I am,
I am not worthy to speak thy name.
You've won my heart Dear Lord,
You take my breath away.
Even in your silence,
I see Your beauty.
From the pinnacle heights
to the lowliest plains.
Throughout my life,
You have shown me Your mercy and grace.
You have given me hope
even in my despair.
You are benevolent
as the sun and moon shows itself
throughout the night and day.
Even in the deepest, darkest skies,
the glistening stars heralds
Your glorious work when they shine.
As this evil world speaks
with an evil tongue,
to deceive the lost.

So shall we speak,

with **'God's Given Words'**

no matter what's the cost.

Very soon,

for a very short time,

evil will take complete control of this world.

It is and always has been a fight between good and evil,

but good will finally prevail.

For now, we are just a dreamer of dreams

of what's to come.

We can only give it to You,

as You will have the final say.

So finally, we have to leave it to you,

as we only can press forward and pray.

IV

What Do I Call You?
'My Psalm To My Lord'

You are more holy,

then my words could ever say.

I try to remind You of that,

every time that I pray.

You are so full of love,

and so much compassion.

To even want to forgive me,

from all of my transgressions.

You pulled me out of the deepest,

depths of a sinful sea.

And that alone,

is a miracle to me.

So, what do I call You Lord,

it's my personal plea?

You're so righteous and true,

so, what word should it be?

You do miracles each day,

for millions to be blessed.

But what name should I call You?

I cannot even guess.

You're loving and caring,

and forgiving that's true.

For that I say a multitude of,

'Thank You'. But that's really not good enough,

as I feel so inept.

My words seem so futile,

as I try not to forget.

Of all of Your ways,

so much wiser than mine.

You are most holy,

and **'Definitely Divine'**.

You have complete control,

of time and of space.

No want-to-be god,

could ever take Your place,

So, what name should I call You,

when I call out in prayer?

Or when I talk to others about You,

with my heart I do bare?

I said it in my first book,

as I look to the stars.

We have no words in our language to say how,

'Great And Awesome That You Are'.

V

A Psalm For Today.

Pastor Keith Cameron D. D.

O God hear the cry of Your people.
There is division in our land.
Use us Your children to be ministers of Your peace.
O Lord God. hear the cry of Your children,
that all lives do matter.
Red and yellow, black and white,
they are precious in Your sight.
O God let us see past our difference,
and see what brings us together.
It is the breath of God,
that is within us that makes us one.
So, help us to see souls of other,
and not the color of their skin.

VI

A Psalm For Today.
Part Two

Pastor Keith Cameron D. D.

O God I ask,

that You release us from our suffering.

As You do demonstrate Your glory,

and draw all people towards You.

Lift this virus from us,

by Your kindness and compassion.

Of God may Your church repent of its' sin,

and rejoice in Your forgiveness.

As we come before You,

with broken hearts to be healed.

It is our prayer,

that You will send a sweeping revival.

That will change our land,

and touch this world.

O God and once again,

may the world know Your mercy.

Let us break with praise,

and shout with our voices,
lifted in songs in every language.
Let every hand be lifted high,
holding one another,
declaring that we are one in the Lord.

VII

The sign of the times
as it talks about in the Bible are near,
as many are still coming to the cross.
As we are not to judge,
we should spread God's word,
and let it be known to the world
that it is true.
The power of darkness is taking more,
and more control of this world each day.
Because of this
people will suffer and die.
They say peace, peace,
but there will be no peace.
This world will never see eternal,
everlasting true peace,
till Jesus comes back,
to rule across this land.

Before I give you mine, and others **'Modern Day Proverbs'**, I would like to give you some of the proverbs from other countries, and then three of my favorite Proverbs out of the Bible.

Proverbs
From
Other
Countries.

1. It's better to light a candle than curse the darkness. Chinese

2. A man who uses force, is afraid of reasoning. Kenyan

3. Examine what is said, not who speaks. Arab

4. A promise is a cloud; fulfillment is rain. Samoa

5. The wallet of the timid man neither increases nor decreases. Malta

6. A stupid act entails doing the work twice over. Burma

7. What you see in yourself, is what you see in the world. Afghanistan

8. When the sun rises, it rises for everyone. Cuban

9. Evil enters like a needle, and spreads like an oak tree. Ethiopian

10. If you go to a donkey's house, don't talk about ears. Jamaican

11. Change yourself, and fortune will change. Portuguese

12. If you fear God, you won't fear humans. Albania

13. Who sieves too much, keeps the rubbish? Belgium

14. A beautiful thing is never perfect. Egyptian

15. No man can paddle two canoes at the same time. Bantu

16. A man does not wander far from where his corn is roasting. Nigeria

17. The heart that loves is always young. Greek
18. There is no shame in not knowing. The shame lies in not finding out. Russian
19. A bird does not sing because it has an answer. It sings because it has a song. Chile
20. An ant on the move does more than a dozing ox. Morocco
21. Turn your face to the sun, and the shadows will fall behind you. New Zealander
22. Whoever gossips to you, will gossip about you. Spanish
23. One spoon of soup in need, has more value than a pot of soup when we have an abundance of food. Angola
24. When the mouse laughs at the cat, there's a hole nearby. Norway
25. If you wish good advice, consult an old man. Romania
26. Speak the truth, but leave immediately after. Slovenian
27. Advise and counsel him. If he does not listen, let adversity teach him. Ethiopia
28. If you want to go fast, go alone. If you want to go far, go together. African

29. Give a man a fish, and you feed him for a day. Teach a man to fish, and you feed him for a lifetime. Chinese

30. Where love reigns, the impossible may be attained. Indian

31. Every disadvantage has its' advantage. Uganda

32. A friendship that dies is never reborn. Belize

33. The hunt is like a dance for men, for the women the dance is the hunt. Austria

34. It takes a whole village to raise a child. African

35. Men who have lost heart, never yet won a trophy. Greece

36. Don't allow the grass to grow on the path of friendship. Vietnam

37. There is no shame in not knowing. The shame lies in not finding out. Russia

38. To be willing, is only half the task. Armenian

39. Tell your friend a lie. If he keeps its' secret, then tell him the truth. Portugal

40. Who begins too much, accomplishes little. German

41. We start as fools, and become wise through experience. Tanzania

42. Beauty lies in the eye of the beholder. English

43. A wise man learns at the fool's expense. Brazil

44. A good laugh and a long sleep, are the best cures in the doctor's book. Ireland

45. Do not protect yourself with a fence, but rather by your friends. Czech Republic

46. Fear not the man who fears God. Saudi Arabia

47. A spoon does not know the taste of soup, nor a learned fool the taste of wisdom. Welsh

48. A dog that barks all the time gets little attention. Argentina

49. Having a good discussion is like having riches. Kenya

50. No one tests the depth of the river with both feet. Ghana

51. There are a thousand paths to every wrong. Poland

52. Two things rule the world, reward and punishment. Bosnia

53. The reputation of a thousand years, may be determined by the conduct of one hour. Japanese

54. Don't bargain for fish, which are still in the water. Iceland

55. Words should be weighed, not counted. Yiddish

56. Wisdom does not come overnight. Somalia

57. Never ask God to give you anything. Ask Him to put you where things are. Mexico

58. Pray that you will never have to bear all that you are able to endure. Jewish

59. Words are like eggs: when they are hatched, they have wings. Lebanon

60. Don't trust in fortune until you are in Heaven. Philippines

61. Still waters run deep. Latin

62. God promises a safe landing, but not a calm passage. Bulgaria

63. Measure a thousand times and cut once. Turkish

64. Fear less, hope more, eat less, chew more, whine less, breathe more, talk less, say more, hate less, love more, and all good things will be yours. Sweden

65. Character is always corrupted by prosperity. Icelandic

66. Beauty and folly are constant companions. Costa Rica

67. Aim high in your career, but stay humble in your heart. South Korea

68. Speech is silver; silence is golden. Switzerland

69. To him that watches, everything is revealed. Italy

70. It's not shameful not to know, but it's shameful not to ask. Azerbaijan

71. You can outdistance that which is running after you, but not what is running inside you. Rwanda

72. A word from the mouth is like a stone from a sling. Spain

73. God does not pay weekly, but He pays at the end. Netherlands

74. A fool is like the big drum that beats fast, but does not realize its' hollowness. Malaysia

75. Better to ask twice, than to lose your way once. Denmark

Proverbs
From
The
Bible

1. Proverbs 3:5 K.J.V.: Trust in the LORD with all your heart, and lean not on your own understanding;
2. Proverbs 22:6 K.J.V. Train up a child in the way he should go: and when he is old, he will not depart from it.
3. Proverbs 1:7 K.J.V. The fear of the LORD is the beginning of knowledge: but fools despise wisdom and instruction.

Modern Day Proverbs

This too, although I felt led to use this title for this section, I am not saying it is on the same level as the Proverbs in the Bible.

I

Words Of Wisdom

Chaplain Leonard Diebold

The wisdom of the world,
produces pride and sin.
The wisdom of the Holy Spirit,
produces humility and righteousness.
Sin is forbidden,
in the peace,
and love,
of Jesus Christ
our Savior.

II

Three Steps Forward

In our life,
if we take
three steps forward,
and no more
than two steps back,
we will always get
ahead in all
of our endeavors.

III

Three Sides To A Story

There are always three sides,
not two to a story.
There would be one side,
then the other.
Now somewhere
between them both,
is the truth.

IV

The Walk

It is not
The talk that we talk,
but rather
the walk,
that we walk.

V

A Person's Love

Love the person,
not what
they do or say,
if it is against
'God's Holy Word'.

VI

In life,
one of the
worst things
we can do,
is to try
to please
everyone.

VII

Inner strength
comes from
reading the Bible,
praying,
serving,
honoring,
and exalting our
Lord Jesus Christ.

VIII

Telling your story
will not save
the world,
but may save
one soul.

IX

Pastor Keith Cameron D. D.

Don't get so busy
that if you meet
yourself coming back,
and don't know
where you have been.

X

Your life
is what you make it,
but the outcome
of that life,
is from the choices
that you make.

XI

Learn from your mistakes,
but be sure to pass on
what you have learned
from those mistakes,
to others.

XII

When the mind overrides
the heart,
you lose compassion.
With compassion only,
you may lose
your destiny.

XIII

A person's value
is not measured
by what it is on this earth.
Their true worth,
is more precious
then diamonds and gold.

XIV

Wishing and daydreaming
serves
no purpose,
as it takes actions,
to complete
all of your challenges.

XV

Wisdom only grows
as you mature.
So wiser is the man
in his old age,
than in his youth.

XVI

You may have
faith in many things,
but if it is not
in God,
the eternal outcome
is fruitless.

XVII

Security and wealth are not
the material things
that you have,
but it is in your
everlasting salvation
with God.

XVIII

In loving people
you may be disappointed,
brokenhearted,
and they may leave you
or die.
Not loving people,
you will find yourself
sad and alone.

XIX

'God's Agape Love'

will always be faithful,

everlasting, and true.

The love

for this world,

will never last.

XX

People who
just make excuses,
are not only
deceiving others,
but telling a lie
to oneself.

People make excuses for not doing something they could have done, or not doing something they should have done. To me, this is of little, or no value. They also make excuses to not take blame for their actions, deeds, or non-actions.

I got this from:

https://www.google.com/search?q=excuses+definition&oq=excuses+definition&aqs=chrome..69i57j0i22i30l7.11480j1j4&sourceid=chrome&ie=UTF-8

Definitions for the word excuses:

1. Attempt to lessen the blame attaching to (a fault or offense); seek to defend or justify.
2. A reason or explanation put forward to defend or justify a fault or offense.

XXI

We cannot take
immoral acts,
to judge are actions or thoughts,
which are against God's word,
and call it politically correct.
To God,
that is just politically wrong.

XXII

We are still the light of this world,
and we should let
that light shine.
Even though
this wicked
and evil world,
is making
it darker,
and darker, each day.

XXIII

Our works,
deeds,
and thoughts,
are feeble and inept,
compared to the
miracles, and mind
of our God.

XXIV

A faithful
man or woman
who does God's work,
is a person
after God's Own Heart.

XXV

Above the floating cloud
is limitless space,
are of things
we cannot see,
or even imagine.

XXVI

As we cannot
change the past,
we can go forward
and unite
a change,
for a better future.

XXVII

There is no greater sacrifice
that we can make,
that is better then serving,
honoring,
and loving,
our Lord Jesus Christ.

XXVIII

The greatest hunger
we should have,
is that
of filling our hearts,
with the knowledge,
and wisdom,
from **'God's Holy Word'**.

XXIX

You can endure the bitter,
but enjoy the sweet.
To mix them,
takes away
the enjoyment
of what you eat,
and what you endure
in life.

XXX

Faith is not in the touch,
nor what thou can see.
Faith is in God,
and that in Him,
you should believe.

XXXI

Trust is not trust,
if
it does not
extend both ways.

XXXII

People who have
special gifts from God,
may make some jealous,
and others
may just not understand.

XXXIII

A promise is not a promise,
if it is contrary
to God's word,
nor ever kept.

XXXIV

As Christians,
sometimes God puts up through
'Trials And Tribulations',
but sometimes
we bring them upon ourselves.

For example, before becoming a Christian I used to smoke. Now because of that I now have chronic-bronchitis which I deal with daily. Just because we became a Christian long after we did what we used to do, does not mean that God will take away the final outcome from what we used to do.

XXXV

Just as the rain cleanses
and nourishes the soil.
So does our tears and laughter,
nourish and cleanse our soul.

Poetry

I

A Gentle Giant

(A tribute to a dear friend who has passed on.)

A gentle giant with a soft-spoken voice,
and now is the time for you to rejoice.
I know through this life you've had
much anguish and pain,
but we know as Christians,
our temporary loss is God's gain.
Your journey through this world
has come to an end,
as ours still have some
twists, turns, and bends.
Well, my dear friend
I do not have much more to say,
till we meet again
one glorious day.
This for sure,
I know you have been
a blessing in my life,
I can truly say that I love you,
my brother in Christ.

II

Snowflakes

Snowflakes how they drift,
from floating clouds in the sky.
The purity and whiteness,
is pleasing to the eye.
In time it changes from what it was,
to turn to water that covers the ground.
That also helps the plant life,
as the circle of life rebounds.
How things can change from what they were,
only God knew how it would finally end.
Starting with just a simple snowflake,
is just one step to help this world to mend.

III

Cry

When I lived upon this earth you hardly called,
nor ever came by.
But now that I have went to a better place,
you say how much you miss me and cry.
You had so many excuses of why
you never stayed in touch,
but they were all a lie.
But now that I am gone,
now you say you miss me and cry.
Do you do it to get the kindness and
sympathy from others,
is that why?
For when others to come around, call, or even send a text,
to console you when you cry?
I do not understand if I ever meant that much to you,
before I left with no good byes.
Now of course you tell others how you're missing me,
as tears come down your eyes.
I can only hope that others don't do to you,
as you have done to me, and living with this lie.
That now, after I am gone you say you care and miss me,

so now is no reason to cry.
My heart still goes out to you,
as I have always loved you and that is why.
I ask you to enjoy the rest of your life,
as for me, don't weep for me and cry.

IV

Faith, Family, Friends,
And Fellowship

Faith is something I hold close to,

as it is the most precious thing I've got.

Along with the salvation that saved my soul,

and that really means a lot.

Next to God, my family means so much to me,

although most of them are gone.

Until I see them when I leave this earth,

sometimes I feel so alone.

My friends mean as much to me,

as all my family did.

Some of my best memories, I remember

with my family though,

was when I was just a kid.

Fellowship is very important to me,

as it fills the loneliness sometimes that I feel.

The kind words, hugs, and love they give,

I know that they are real.

So, when I sum up all,

of what I just said

It can make my life

feel more complete.

But all of this combined in my life will not compare,

when I bow down to Jesus in Heaven,

sitting in **'His Holy Seat'**.

I Love You My Lord Jesus.

V

Crown

They say at least we get one crown or more,

to take to Heaven when Jesus we meet.

I know they were nothing, I would

have ever deserved and took,

if it wasn't for me putting them at **'Jesus' Feet'**.

If I had to pick one, I'd pick the **'Crown Of Thorns'**,

instead of putting it on my Christ.

He lived such a righteous life, and died for my sins,

while many times I did not do what was right.

So not much to say, about all of those crowns,

that we lay at **'Jesus' Feet'**.

He's the One, Who deserves all those crowns,

that through His death, our sins that He did defeat.

So, what can I say as I go away,

of my life that Jesus has touched.

Again, if I could say every **'Micro-second'** of each day,

'That I Love You Jesus' so much.

VI

The Old Rugged Cross

It was that old rugged cross,
or have we just forgot?
Of all the rejection, pain, and suffering,
about Jesus that was once taught.
How they persecuted and rejected Him,
and called Him a fraud.
And then hung Him on a cross,
this most righteous **'Son of God'**.
Please think hard
of how this could ever be,
of how Jesus only came down to earth,
to only just to set us free.
Although we are underserving,
He cleansed us all from sins.
Shedding His blood for our salvation,
for our souls that He could win.
Some call it **'Good Friday'**,
for our debt in which He paid.
But was not good for Him,
for upon that cross of which He did lay.
Forgiveness of our sins is priceless,

of which one could not afford.

But only something that could be done,

by **'Jesus Christ Our Lord'**.

If you knew the true meaning of the word Easter,

it should be a word you should not say.

But more appropriately should be called,

'His Resurrection Day'.

You see Jesus came out of that tomb,

called a grave, and from that **'He Was Risen'**.

For three days He was considered dead,

His human life back to Him was given.

The Bible tells you the full story,

better than I am able to give.

Of the true life of Jesus,

and how He did live.

So, take this time of year,

as to not forget what He did.

Because of that He suffered and died,

so through eternity with Him we shall live.

VII

Splinter Vs. Tree

I remember how I felt when I was a kid,
when a splinter got into me.
Now I think of all the pain Jesus suffered,
laying on that horrible tree.
When my dad stuck that needle into me,
you could really hear me yell.
Nothing like the pain that Jesus felt,
laying against that cross with all of those whelps.
When the splinter was out, and I saw a little blood,
the crying did begin.
But Jesus lost all of His blood,
it was to save us from all of our sins.
I know the pain for Him was so much worse,
than that little splinter was in me.
I'm so glad I was not there,
to see Him hanging from that tree.
I'm so glad He took that tree,
instead of a little splinter in Him.
Because had He not did that,
we never would have,
been saved from all of our sins.

VIII

Help Me Jesus

Help me, help me Jesus,
I'm not sure what to do.
I'm feel so lost and lonely in my life,
ever since I strayed from You.
Please forgive me for putting You out of my life,
is there still a chance for a sinner like me?
Or am I destined to walk, this earth without You,
please hear **'My Sincere Plea'**.
I'm sorry, oh so sorry,
can you find forgiveness in your heart?
My life was going so good with You,
please give me a second start.
As I was weeping on my knees,
trying to decide now what to do.
I thought I heard a soft voice say,
"You may have left Me, but I never left you!"

IX

Drop

Did you ever drop something just like I did,
and wondered if you're losing your touch?
Or see drops of rain fall on the ground,
but like today I think it fell down too much.
Or a drop of snow, when it first comes down,
without the cold it sure does look fine.
When it piles up and the sun is out,
you'll see it **'Glistens And Shines'**.
The word drop has been used, in so many ways,
like the hint to someone you have dropped.
Or in a restaurant to hear some music,
in a jukebox a quarter you pop.
With many of my poems, where I'm going with that,
truthfully, I usually in advance do I know.
Just now it finally came into my mind,
let's talk about that snow.
It looks so white, pure, and pretty to see,
that I want you all to know.
But much whiter, purer, with nothing to see,
is when Jesus cleanses our soul.

X

Joke

I'd like to tell you a joke that I heard,
if only I could truly remember.
One thing that I know, that it was was quite funny,
but now my mind is in kind of a blur.
From all the poems I've written before,
I hope it did not slip my mind.
It started like this... ah, no... maybe not,
I hope I can think of it in time.
One thing I remember, it was very funny,
and unlike most jokes it did rhyme.
The biggest thing now, that I'm worried about,
is maybe I'm just losing my mind.
I just think I'll give up, and go out to do an errand,
I hope you can forgive me please.
As I finally remembered, on how it went,
it really wasn't that funny to me.

XI

What A Beautiful Day

What a beautiful day it is,
to see the birds and hear them sing.
To see all of **'God's Beauty'**,
as you can hear the school bell ring.
You see a deer with two young babies,
as they run through the woods.
And watch the sun as it comes up,
while driving through the backwoods.
You see the mountains, rivers, and beautiful trees,
and the flowers still in bloom.
You smile as you see all of these,
as you get to your destination soon.
As you get out of your car,
the people you meet are so nice.
And all the wondrous things you saw today,
you cannot put on it a price.
But now that you're at your destination,
and those thoughts will soon be robbed.
As you slowly enter into those doors,
of your lousy, stinking job.

XII

A Man Called Legion

There was a man they called **'Legion'**,
who was possessed by many demons,
he never had a choice of what he would do.
I'm sure he rather not live the life he was living,
with those creatures in him, that
were like some bad shrews.
He lived in the tombs, naked both day and night,
almost nothing he couldn't do.
When they chained him up, to keep him under control,
there was nothing he couldn't break through.
Just like a fairy tale, that had a happy ending,
all those were lies, but this one we know is true.
But a man we call **'Jesus'** came out of a boat,
to the possessed man of which He came to.
First out of that boat, He didn't take long,
to meet a man who had a lost soul.
But the demons inside him, knew Who Jesus was,
but that man whom they lived in didn't know.
Jesus said: *"Hi"*, to greet that guy,
but the demons did all the talking you bet.
They said: *"Jesus it's not our time, for our demise,*

please don't send us to hell, not yet!"
Jesus said: *"What do you want me to do?*
There's no way I will leave you in this man."
So all those demons thought, they
thought, and they thought.
and they said: *"Jesus we came up with a plan.*
Just look over there, to those pigs on that slope,
and put us into those swine."
So, Jesus honored their request,
and with Him it didn't take much time.
Pigs are some of the nastiest animals on this earth,
who will eat anything.
So, when those demons entered those swine,
even pigs wanted nothing to do with those things.
The pigs ran and not walked, down that steep slope,
they'd rather die than have those creatures in them.
So, the man now without, those demons in him,
I'll bet he laughed with one big grin.
Of all the poems that I wrote, and some for a joke,
definitely this one has a moral.
I hope that you know, that those demons will,
soon find themselves in a place called hell.
Now I sure do suggest, that you think about this,
a pig may be smarter than we think.
They wanted to live no more, with
those evil spirits in them,

they'd rather die, so they took their last drink.
Are some of us not, much smarter than swine,
or are we maybe just confused?
If the nasty pigs don't want them, then why should we,
where in eternity with them you'll be abused.
So now it's time, to finally make up your mind,
like the swine did, who died with those demons.
So now you have, an important decision to make,
if you make the right one like the pigs you should run.
To the altar and down on your knees,
to ask God for forgiveness of your sins.
Now that's the first start, to getting apart,
away from all those demons.
So now you won't live, with all those evil beings,
that even a pig wanted to live without.
Now do you believe, we can always learn,
even from swine with one big snout.

XIII

Blue Skies

Do you look out and see the **'Deep Blue Skies'**,
but anticipate the storms?
Maybe go out and feel the warm summer breeze,
or feel the burst of a terrible wind coming on.
Maybe in the morning you see the dew that glistens,
or feel that a major rain will soon arrive?
Can you see the **'Son That Shines'** upon you,
or really bad weather that seems alive?
Our life can be just like that,
if we just don't look for all those **'Sonny Days'**.
Or that someday, something bad will happen,
that makes you feel your life's always on a cloudy day.
Just look around and be grateful,
and try not to be so blue.
And let the **'Son Shine'** of the **'Son Of The Father'**,
'Shine Down Always Upon You'!

XIV

Star's Light Star's Bright

Star's light, stars in the night,
as I look upon them, they seem so small and bright.
As they look so far into the night,
I cannot wait to see **'God's Holy Light'**.
The Bible says with God there will be no sun needed,
and in Heaven there will be no night.
The **'Luminous Light Of God'**,
will be all that we need.
As I find this from,
the **'Scriptures Of God'** that I read.
As I leave you with
these **'Passages From God'**.
It talks about **'God's Pure Light'**
in the future we'll see from above.

1 John 1:5 N.I.V.: This is the message we have heard from Him and declare to you: God is light; in Him there is no darkness at all.

Revelation 22:5 N.I.V.: There will be no more night. They will not need the light of a lamp or the light of the sun, for the Lord God will give them light. And they will reign for ever and ever.

XV

One Nation Under God.

One **'Nation Under God'**,
was how this nation was formed.
Following **'His Laws And Commandments'**,
is how it was born.
Never should we sway from **'His Word'**,
nor lose sight of **'His Love'**.
Our actions and deeds,
should come from **'Heaven Above'**.
It seems that we swayed.
and now follow the laws of man.
God was the one who gave us commandments and laws,
to rule this glorious land.
It's time to decide now,
if we'll follow man's unholy rod.
Or shall be once again be considered,
'One Nation Under God'.

XVI

The Darkness Grows Darker

As this world grows more evil and wicked,
as to put it in the dark.
We are the light of this world,
where we are to leave our mark.
Don't let the evilness take over,
and we should continue to let our light shine.
Always show the **'Agape Love Of God'**,
and be ever so kind.
The darkness of the world will finally leave,
after the **'Great Tribulation'**.
For then Jesus will return to this earth,
to make this world **'One Great Nation'**.
So never fret, nor ever regret,
to let your light shine upon this land.
We were never born, nor should we die,
from following the rules of man.
So, one last piece of advice,
as we are living upon this evil and dark earth.
We always have, and ever will be,
a glimmering light since our rebirth.
(Our rebirth is when we finally got saved,
in the name of Jesus Christ.)

XVII

Dear Lord My God

A song I wrote with music on You Tube. To see and hear it, please go to the site below, and leave a comment in the comment section on the bottom left of the song.

https://www.youtube.com/
watch?v=b90A8RcLRpc&feature=youtu.be

Dear Lord my God,
I search for answers.
For my soul is troubled,
of the future of this land.
Of all the tragedies,
that will be done by man.
Though these thoughts,
which made me cry,
but in my prayers,
I sensed You nearby.

On one summer day,
You sent a shiver through me.
It felt like the coolness,
of a fall-like-breeze.

Then through one lonely cloud,

You sent a pouring rain.

In my broken heart I wondered,

what could it mean?

I felt they were tears,

from Your sadness and love.

My heart still bleeds,

cause we abort the lives of unborn babes.

For they are now,

sent to an early grave.

And for those who suffered and died,

for not denying, but loving You.

Although, I do not,

understand.

Somehow I know,

it was not Your plan.

To think You had,

to give Your life for the lost,

with 2 pieces of wood,

three iron spikes to make Your cross.

Most people do not understand,

what You did it for.

Please repent,

if all this evil does not stop,

the Great Tribulation,
will be knocking at our door.

Dear Lord my God,
I'm still in wonder.
Just how long on earth,
Your saints will wander.
As my heart cries out,
yes, I still ponder.
When Your return,
please wait no longer.
As I know,
Your time,
is soon.

XIII

The Red, The White, And The Blue

The red, the white, and the blue,
that people have lived and died for.
It represents the God Who gave us this land,
the One we should follow and adore.
The red stood for the blood that was shed,
to help to make us free.
The white represents the God we serve,
Who is righteous with purity?
The color blue can symbolize
serenity, stability, wisdom, or inspiration.
Which helps keep our freedom,
of this nation.
So next time
you see our red, white, and blue,
make sure you pay tribute,
for its' honor is due.

XIX

A Warm And Glorious Day

It is a warm and glorious day,
each day I serve my Lord.
He is the One through His death
we are restored.
No other name can give us
eternal life.
No other name can help us
through our struggles and strife.
The name of Jesus Christ
we should loudly proclaim.
That is only He would can save us,
as there is be no other name.

XX

Thunder And Lightning

There is thunder and lightning,
that most of you do not here.
It may be from the wrath of God,
because so many do not care.
On our money it says,
'In God We Trust'.
They keep printing money with nothing to back it,
so our economy could go bust.
I can hear God's voice,
it's like thunder in my ears.
And what He is saying,
is filling my heart with tears.
Lightning yes,
the lightning may not be from God at all.
But with all the bad that is happening,
even if not His wrath,
the way this this nation is going,
it will fall.

XXI

Murder In The First Degree

As I've said it before and I'll say it again,
'Abortion Is Murder In The First Degree'!
Are you that ignorant, or just that plain dumb,
that it is something you cannot see?
It says in the Bible,
that we are not to call someone a Fool.
And we're brought up with those ethics,
of the **'Golden Rule'**.
'To do unto others, as they
would do unto you',
do you even know what that means?
You're doing the work of that mean old devil,
in fulfilling one of his evil schemes.
As the Bible tells me not to call someone a **'FOOL'**,
I will take my chance with Him.
(Him is God.)
So whoever came up with this stupid idea you Fool,
you just gave Satan a grin.
'Murder Is A Sin' in the **'Ten Commandments'**,
in the Bible it is **'Number Six'**.
You Fool, you Fool, you such **'SILLY FOOLS'**,

when will these **'Unjust Murders'** ever quit?

You are doing the devil's work you Fool,

can't you just see that?

One day you will answer for all of those

crimes to an **'Almighty God'**,

and **'THAT TRULY IS A FACT'**!

My God may not be happy with

me calling you a **'FOOL'**,

but that is a chance I will take.

I know He's more concerned of those

'Precious Lives You Destroy',

than any criticism that I could make.

What a Fool that you are, I will not discard,

that I still think that you're a Fool, that's true.

If you don't change your ways, it will soon come that day,

that my God may be calling you that too.

If you don't get saved, before you go to the grave,

that's when your troubles will really begin.

At the **'Great White Throne**

Judgement Of God',

where He'll lay down all of your sins.

He'll send you to **'HELL'** to live for eternity,

what I'm telling you is what I know that is true.

But I got good news, but it's only for me,

that I'll not be standing next to you.

You'll still have that chance while you'll still alive,

to find **'God's Amazing Grace'**.

Quit what you're doing and get on your knees,

to ask God for His forgiveness for you to be saved.

But for all of you, who won't quit what you do,

you Fool, you Fool, you **'STUPID FOOL'**.

When you go to **'HELL'**, with that devil that you'll serve,

you'll find him to be very cruel.

So, stop your murdering of those **'Children of God'**,

cause **'He's The One'** you'll finally have to answer to.

Cause all those babies you're murdering

will all go to Heaven,

So, what if those babies had the

choice of you living or dying,

what do you think that they should do?

Would you want them to let you live or die,

or do you even have a clue?

So you Fool, you Fool, you such **'SILLY FOOLS'**,

you must pick the master that you want to serve.

Will it be the **'Holy God In Heaven'**,

or the one doing the havoc upon this earth?

(That is Satan.)

As for me I'll serve the God above,

so take what I tell for what it is worth.

Would you rather serve **'Jesus Christ Our Savior'**,

or the demons who have a lot of control on this earth?

So, to all you **'FOOLS'** of this world as I do close,

you still have time to change your minds.

Will it be **'Heaven Or Hell'** for you, what will you do, because you do not have much time?

P.S. Don't you understand that aborting babies is just **'Madness'**? You see the devil knows once you kill those babies that they will automatically be going to **'Heaven'**. So, think about this, whose soul do you think he is after with the killing of such innocent lives? If you still do not understand say **'Bingo'** you won. But what is it that you won? It is a one-way ticket to a place called **'HELL'**. So, is this truly the prize you would want to win? So take a deep breath, while you are still living to make the right choice. Not the choice that it is alright to kill all those newborns. **'WHICH IS WRONG IN GOD'S EYES!'** But **'Your Free Will Choice'** is: If you want to change from those wicked ways and finally **'STOP'** from being involved in this insanity that is still going on in sacrificing these **'Precious Young Children'**. So, my last words to you is to stop being a **'FOOL'** with Satan as your leader, and make the two right choices, and best choices you could ever make.

1. Choice of letting these **'Newborns Live'**.
2. Choice of where you would rather live. Will it be **'Heaven'**, or a dreaded place we call **'Hell'**. Please make the right one. **'YOUR CALL!'**

XXII

To Honor Those We Have Loss

To honor those
that we have loss.
Those who have served, and died,
serving Him on the cross.
He is the One,
Who died for our sins.
So that our souls,
He would win.
Jesus Christ is His name,
there is no other.
Matthew 12:50 says:
that He is our Brother.

XXIII

That's Not My Job!

Author unknown

This is a story about four people named
Everybody, Somebody, Anybody and Nobody.

There was an important job to be done,
and Everybody was sure,
that Somebody would do it.
Anybody could have done it,
but Nobody did it.
Somebody got angry about that,
because it was Everybody's job.
Everybody thought
Anybody could do it,
but Nobody realized,
that Everybody wouldn't do it.
It ended up that Everybody
blamed Somebody,
when Nobody
did what Anybody
could have done.

XXIV

Dusty Bible

Is there dust on your Bible,
just lying in the other room?
You say that you never have time to read it,
or at least that is what you assume.
You are not kidding me,
just trying to kid yourself.
So, take the time to read it,
that precious book,
just lying on your shelf.

XXV

Fiery Darts

Do you feel those fiery darts,
coming at you from all sides?
Sometimes they are trials by fire,
that you feel deep down inside.
It is the devil who throws
those fiery darts at you.
In order to test your faith,
and now I'll give you a clue.
Today you must decide who you'll serve,
as you can only have one master not two.
Will it be Satan you serve,
or Jesus Who is faithful and true.

Matthew 6:24 K.J.V.: No man can serve two masters: for either he will hate the one, and love the other; or else he will hold to the one, and despise the other. Ye cannot serve God and mammon.

Revelation

Warning

Woe to those who sin in this evil and wicked world. If they do not change from their wicked ways and repent, in time, they will feel the wrath, and eternal judgement, of God. This is called: **'The Great White Throne Judgement.'**

Revelation 20:11-15 K.J.V.: And I saw a great white throne, and Him that sat on it, from whose face the earth and the heaven fled away; and there was found no place for them. And I saw the dead, small and great, stand before God; and the books were opened: and another book was opened, which is the book of life: and the dead were judged out of those things which were written in the books, according to their works. The sea gave up the dead who were in it, and Death and Hades delivered up the dead who were in them. And they were judged, each one according to his works. Then Death and Hades were cast into the lake of fire. This is the second death. And whosoever was not found written in the book of life was cast into the lake of fire.

Later I will tell you how to get saved, and also prayers you can use to afford this from happening to you. Beware of what this book tells you then, because it may be the last chance you have, for you to be saved. No one knows when the time of their death will occur. Scripture says:

Ecclesiastes 7:17 E.S.V.: Be not overly wicked, neither be a fool. Why should you die before your time?

Ecclesiastes 3:2 E.S.V.: A time to be born, and a time to die; a time to plant, and a time to pluck up what is planted;

James 4:14 E.S.V.: Yet you do not know what tomorrow will bring. What is your life? For you are a mist that appears for a little time and then vanishes.

Hebrews 9:27 E.S.V.: And just as it is appointed for man to die once, and after that comes judgment.

Romans 6:23 E.S.V.: For the wages of sin is death, but the free gift of God is eternal life in Christ Jesus our Lord.

Just Jokin'

1. It is better for people to think you are foolish, then open your mouth and relieve all doubt.

2. My wife says I have only two faults. One I do not listen to her, and some other thing that she mentioned.

3. How much better would life be if a liar's pants did catch on fire.

4. Many islands I have been too said that it was their island that Christopher Columbus discovered in 1492. I guess he just didn't want to stop to ask for directions.

5. I just thought about this. Those who try to scam you seem to never call on weekends. They must have a union.

6. Age 60 may be the new 40, but 9:00 P.M. is the new midnight.

7. I hate it when a couple argues in public, and I missed the beginning, and don't know whose side I'm on.

8. When someone asks what I did over the weekend, I squirm and asked: *"Why, what did you hear?"*

9. Don't bother walking a mile in my shoes. That would be boring. Spend 30 seconds in my head. That'll scare you.

10. Sometimes, someone unexpected comes into your life out of nowhere, makes your heart race, and changes you forever. We call those people cops.

11. To pro athletes who think we're listening to you, if I wanted advice from someone good at chasing a ball, I'd rather listen to a dog.

12. Once you understand why the pizza is made round, and packed in a square box, and then eaten in a triangle, then you'll understand women.

13. I met a woman outside the mall crying. She said she lost $200, so I gave her $40 of the $200 I have just found. When God blesses you, you must bless others.

14. Charley, a new retiree-greeter at Wal-Mart, just couldn't seem to get to work on time. Every day he was 5, 10, 20 minutes late. But he was a good worker, really tidy, clean-shaven, sharp-minded and a real credit to the company, and obviously demonstrated their **'Older Person Friendly'** policies. One day the boss called him into the office for a talk. *"Charley, I have to tell you, I like your work ethics, you do a bang-up job when you finally come to work, but your being late so often is quite bothersome."* Charlie: *"Yes sir, I know, and I am working on it."* Boss: *"Well good, you are a team player. That's what I like to hear."* Charlie: *"Yes sir,*

I understand your concern, and I will try harder." Seeming puzzled, the manager went on to say, *"It is odd though, you coming in late. I know you are retired from the Armed Forces. What did they say to you if you showed up in the morning so late and so often?"* The old man looked down at the floor, and then smiled. He chuckled quietly, then said with a grin, *"They usually saluted and said: Good morning General, can I get you coffee sir?"*

15. As I am getting older, I have so many unanswered questions. I still have not found out who let the Dogs Out...Where's the beef...How to get to Sesame Street... Why Dora doesn't just use Google Maps... Why do all flavors of fruit loops taste exactly the same, or how many licks does it take to get to the center of a tootsie pop......Why eggs are packaged in a flimsy paper carton, but batteries are secured in plastic that's tough as nails, yet light bulbs too are in a flimsy carton... Ever buy scissors? You need scissors to cut into the packaging of scissors... I still don't understand why there is Braille on drive up ATM's or why **'Abbreviated'** is such a long word, or why is there a D in **'Fridge'** but not in refrigerator... Why lemon juice is made with artificial flavor yet dish-washing liquid is made with real lemons... Why they sterilize the needle

for lethal injections... and, why do you have to put your two cents in, but it's only a penny for your thought. Where's that extra penny going... Why do The Alphabet Song and Twinkle Twinkle Little Star have the same tune...? Why did you just try to sing those two previous songs... and just what is Victoria's secret? .... Well, I know that answer...What would you do for a Klondike bar and you know as soon as you bite into it, it falls apart...Why do we drive on Parkways and park on Driveways? Do you really think I am this witty? ... I got this from a friend, who stole it from her brother's girlfriend's, uncle's cousin's, baby momma's doctor, who lived next door to an old class mate's mail man.

16. Mark A. decided to run for president in a small African nation. He went to every tribe in that nation to campaign for that position. Problem is, that almost every tribe he went to, he needed a translator. After spending three weeks on the road sharing his views, of what he will do if he gets elected as president to each tribe, he finally reached his final destination. Luckily enough, the chieftain of that tribe was his translator. After he completed each sentence of how he would improve their country, and the head of the tribe translated,

you could hear the crowd scream and shout *"Bula, Bula"*. After about twenty minutes, he finished his speech. Every time that the chieftain would translate what he had said, the crowd would always shout with excitement *"Bula, Bula"*. After all was said and done, Mark A. asked the chief if he could see those sacred cows he had talked about earlier. The chief said: *"Fine, but do not step in the Bula, Bula."*

17. This is a true story, that I hope you will find as funny as I did. When I was a child in Kansas City, whenever there was even a little bit of snow, my dad would be out cleaning the sidewalk and driveway. Much later, when I was in my thirties, when I went to visit my dad, and there was maybe six inches of snow, nothing was done. I asked my dad about why when I was a kid, he would be shoveling snow when there was only a little, and now when there is six inches or more, he does not touch it. His reply to me was: *"I changed my way of doing things son. I figured mother nature put it there, then mother nature can take it away."*

18. I just saw on the news, that they said that because of the cold weather that people should check on the elderly. I get up about 7 A.M., bring donuts and coffee.

19. A pessimist sees a dark tunnel, while an optimist sees the light at the end of a tunnel. A realist sees a freight train, while the locomotive engineer sees three fools standing on the track.

20. My goal for 2020 was to lose 20 pounds. Now in 2021, I only have 28 pounds to go.

21. I ate a salad for dinner. Mostly tomatoes, and croutons. It was one large crouton with cheese and tomatoes. Fine then, it was a pizza.

22. Children really do not realize how easy they have it. When I was a child, I had to walk over ten feet to change the television set.

23. In my old age I learn something every day, and forget a half-a-dozen others.

24. In my younger years, I may not have been good in sports, nice looking, talented or very smart. I forget where I was going with this.

25. Wife: *"What would you do if I died? Would you get remarry again?"*

Husband: *"No."*

Wife: *"Why not? Don't you like being married to someone?"*

Husband: *"Of course, I do."*

Wife: *"Then why wouldn't you want to remarry?"*

Husband: *"Ok, I would get married again"*

Wife: *"Would you live in this house with your new wife?"*

Husband: *"Yes, there is nothing wrong with this home."*

Wife: *"Would you let her drive my van?"*

Husband: *"Yes, it's almost new, and we are still making payments on it."*

Wife: *"Would you let her wear my jewelry?"*

Husband: *"No, I am sure she would have her own."*

Wife: *"Would she play with my golf clubs?"*

Husband: *"No, she is left-handed."*

Wife: (She is silent.)

Husband: (I will let you decide what funny comment you would want to make on this one.)

More Humor That I Just Found

1. Families are like fudge...mostly sweet, with just a few nuts.

2. The four stages of a man's life:
You believe in Santa Claus.
You don't believe in Santa Claus.
You are Santa Claus.
You look like Santa Claus.

3. Dumb Blonde Joke: Last year I replaced all the windows in my house with those expensive double-pane energy-efficient kind. Yesterday, I got a call from the contractor who installed them. He was complaining that the windows had been installed a whole year ago, and I hadn't paid for them yet. Now just because I'm blonde doesn't mean that I am stupid. So, I told him just exactly what his fast-talking sales person had told me a year ago. That in just one year those windows would pay for themselves! *"Hello."* (I told him). *"It's been a year."* There was only silence at the other end of the line, so I finally just hung up. He hasn't called back. I'll bet he felt stupid.

4. A man and a woman were traveling on a train. Woman: *"Every time you smile, I feel like inviting you to my place."* Man: *"Are you single?"* Woman: *"No, I am a dentist."*

5. 8 A.M.: Too tired to think. Noon: Too tired to think. 5 P.M.: Too tired to think. Midnight: I wonder how dragons blow out candles? This one you may have to think about, or ask a friend to explain.

6. A married couple had gotten into an argument, and for many days had not been talking to one another. Instead, they were passing notes back and forth. One evening the husband walked up to the wife and handed her a note that said, Wake me up tomorrow at 6 A.M. in the morning. When he woke up the next morning it was 9 A.M... He immediately got angry with his wife and turned around to speak to her, but then he noticed a note on her pillow which said: **"Wake up, it is 6."**

7. Husband and his wife had a fight. In tears his wife decided to call her mom and said: *"He fought with me again today, and I am coming to live with you."* The mom replied: *"No, he must pay for his arguing, so I am coming to live with you."*

Funny
Quotes
From
Kids

1. Never trust your dog to watch your food.

2. Never try to baptize a cat.

3. Felt markers are not good to use as lipstick.

4. If you want a kitten, start asking for a horse.

5. The young, and even the old may appreciate my sense of humor. When I have not seen someone for a while, I ask them to face the wall and say: *"Glad to see your back."*

6. Also, I have been known to call someone on the last day of the year, and call back the next day and say: *"How the world have you been doing? I haven't talked to you since last year."*

7. I don't see the point of exercising. I get enough exercise by pushing my luck, jumping to conclusions and flying off the handle. Surely that's plenty.

8. When your Mom is mad at your Dad, don't let her brush your hair.

9. If your sister hits you, don't hit her back. They always catch the second person.

10. Never ask your 3-year-old brother to hold a tomato.

Interesting
Facts

1. Infants are born with approximately 300 bones, but as they grow, some of them fuse together. When they are an adult, they only have 206 bones.
2. Over half of the bones in your body are located in the hands, wrists, feet, and ankles.
3. Every second, your body produces 25 million new cells. In 15 seconds, you will have produced more cells than there are people in the United States.
4. The largest bone in your body is the thigh bone. The smallest is the stirrup, which is inside your ear drum.
5. There is between 60,000-100,000 miles of blood vessels in your body. If they were lay them end-to-end, they would be long enough to travel around the world more than three times.
6. Teeth are considered part of the skeletal system, but are not bones.
7. Accounting for 2% of our body mass, the brain uses 20% of our oxygen and blood supply.
8. Humans are not the biggest, fastest, or strongest animals around, we are the best at something called long distance running. Our long legs, upright posture, and ability to shed heat via sweat are all factors that make us good runners. Early humans used to hunt their prey by chasing it for

long periods of time until the animals literally died from exhaustion.

9. Almost 60% of your body is made up of water.

10. Pound for pound, your bones are stronger than steel. A block of bone, the size of a matchbox can support up to 18,000 pounds of weight.

Funny, But Maybe Corny, Jokes

I found these jokes to be quite funny. Some may be corny, but I still think they are funny.

1. What happens if you get scared to death two times?

2. Is there ever a day that mattresses are not on sale?

3. This is my step ladder, as I never knew my real ladder.

4. If your car is running, I will not vote for it.

5. Frog parking only, as all others will be toad.

6. You can check yourself in to the Hokey Pokey clinic, and turn yourself around.

7. I would like to grow my own food, but where can I find bacon seeds?

8. This is a joke better said then read. I heard this joke decades ago and it definitely is a good Christmas joke. Rudolph The Red, as they called him, lived in Communist Red Russia. He was married to a lady named Natasha. And this is how the argument began. Natasha: *"Rudolph, looks like it is snowing outside."* Rudolph: (As he goes to the window and looks out.) *"No Natasha, that is rain."*
   Natasha: (As she looks out again.) *"No Rudolph, I am sure that is snow."*
   Rudolph: (As he takes a final look, and gets mad at her and says.) *"Rudolph The Red knows (nose) rain (rein) dear (deer)."*

9. One crow speaking to another. First crow: *"You were out all night, and you could not caw once?*

I cawed, and cawed you, and you would not even answer." Second crow: "I tweeted."

10. Husband: My wife is missing. She went shopping yesterday and has not come home!

Officer: "Age?"

Husband: "I'm not sure. Somewhere between 50 and 60. We don't do birthdays."

Officer: "Height?"

Husband: "Maybe a little over five-feet tall."

Officer: "Weight?"

Husband: "Don't know. Not slim, not really fat."

Officer: "Color of eyes?"

Husband: "Sort of brown, I think."

Officer: "Color of hair?"

Husband: "Changes a couple times a year. Maybe dark brown. I can't remember."

Officer: "What was she wearing?"

Husband: *"Could have been pants, or possible a skirt or shorts. I don't know exactly."*

Officer: *"What kind of car did she go in?"*

Husband: *"She went in my truck."*

Officer: *"What kind of truck was it?"*

Husband: *"A 2017, manufactured September 16th, pearl white Ram Limited 494, with 6.4l Hemi V8 engine ordered, with the Ram Box bar and fridge, L.E.D. lighting, back up and front camera. Moose hide leather, heated and cooled seats, with climate-controlled air conditioning. It has a custom matching white cover for the bed, Weather Tech floor mats. Trailing package with gold hitch, sunroof, D.V.D. with full G.P.S. navigation, satellite radio, Cobra 75 W.X.S.T., 40-channel C.B. radio, six cup holders, 3 U.S.B. ports, and 4 power outlets. I recently added special alloy wheels and off-road Toyo tires. It has custom retracting running boards and under-glow wheel well lighting."*

At this point the husband started choking up.

Officer: *"Take it easy sir, we'll find your truck."*

Old Sayings, And How They Came About

1. Am I My Brother's Keeper came about when God asked Cain where his brother Abel was after he killed him. That was his response back to God, although God already knew what had happened.

2. Bite The Bullet came about before they had anything to put a soldier to sleep before an operation, they would have them bite a bullet.

3. One of the ways believed that the word Gringo came about, was possibly that the United States military wore the green outfits a while back when they were in Puerto Rico and the locals did not want them there. They used to say **'Green Go Home'** meaning they wanted the Americans to leave their country, and later shortened to Gringo.

4. Born With a Silver Spoon In Their Mouth meant that when they were born, the godparents were to give a silver spoon to the parents for the baby with they were christened, but if the family was already rich, then they used this expression.

5. Eat Drink And Be Merry came from the scripture Ecclesiastes 8:15.

6. Rule Of Thumb was called that because back in the 17th century, a man in England was allowed to beat his wife with a stick as long as it was not bigger than his thumb.

7. The Blind Leading The Blind expression came from Matthew 15:14.

8. Years ago there was, and still is, a saying *"It Is What It is"*. Do you think that was something new? Many years back, I watched a movie about Scrooge. It was a black and white movie, maybe done in the 1940's. One comment that still sticks to my mind, is that the ghost of the past said: *"It Was what It Was."*

9. Bitter End came from being the last piece of anchor cable for a boat. So, if you let out the cable to the bitter end and there was nothing else you could do to reach the floor of the ocean to hold the ship in place, then you had reached the bitter end.

10. Baker's Dozen actually meant 13. Some bakers were thought to have baked their products with less weight than it should have been, and they were punished for doing so, so they added one more to compensate in case that should happened.

11. Crocodile Tears had a strange meaning. Supposedly the crocodile cried insincerely when it killed and ate a man.

12. The Cat Got Your Tongue, had two possible origins meaning to remain silent unless someone asks you to speak. One of the two possible reasons that

this expression came about, was in ancient Egypt, where liars tongue was cut off and fed to the cats.

13. Flying Colors, meant that when a fleet won a clear victory, the ships would sail back to port with their colors proudly flying from their masts

14. Doubting Thomas, came from the scripture John 20:24-27.

15. Don't Look A Gift Horse In The Mouth, was that you could tell its' age by looking at its' teeth, but this expression came about, if it is a gift you should not look too closely at it, and be glad that someone gave it to you.

16. More Than You Can Shake A Stick At, would be more than you can handle. This became a saying when sheep farmers had more sheep than they could control with their stick.

17. Beat Around The Bush, was something hunters would do to get their prey out of the bushes. Later it became an expression meaning to get straight to the point.

18. The Walls Have Ears, means to be careful when you speak, as someone may be listening to that conversation. Louvre Palace in France, was believed to have a network of listening tubes to discover political secrets and plots.

19. Fly In The Ointment, came from the Bible in Ecclesiastes 10:1.

20. No Spring Chicken, means they have lost their youth. It seems that farmers would get a better price for chickens born in the spring, although farmers would still try to sell the chickens that lived through the winter for the same price. I am guessing that the ones who were born and made it through the winter were tougher to eat.

21. Escape By The Skin Of Your Teeth, came about from Job 19:20.

22. Bury The Hatchet, means to quit fighting, and find some means to a reconciliation. Puritans and Native Americans men would bury their weapons when trying to negotiate a settlement in a dispute.

23. Knowing The Ropes, was an expression used by sailors, saying you should know how to tie all their different types of knots that they used. It means knowing how to do a job properly.

24. Holier Than Thou, was taken from Isaiah 65:5.

25. Cold Feet, is to mean that you have lost your confidence. It came about when soldiers who had frozen feet were not allowed to fight.

26. A Lamb To The Slaughter, was from Isaiah 53:7.

27. A Leopard Not Being Able To Change Its' Spots, came from Jeremiah 13:23.

28. Big Wig, means someone of importance. During the 18th century, politicians used to wear big wigs.

29. Feet Of Clay, was taken from scripture Daniel 2:27-44.

30. Go The Extra Mile was from Matthew 5:41.

31. Hiding Your Light Under A Bushel, was from Matthew 15:15.

32. Caught Red-Handed, means that someone was caught doing something wrong. The expression started when someone was caught butchering an animal that was not his, and if its' blood was on his hands, he would be punished.

33. Once In A Blue Moon, means something rare as a blue moon only happens every 2.7 years.

34. Lock Stock And Barrel, was because there were three parts to the old rifles, the firing mechanism, the stock, and the barrel. Basically, it means all of something.

35. A Long Shot expression was because of the guns of the past were good at short ranges, but if you hit your target farther away is how it got that name.

36. Raining Cats And Dogs, means raining really hard. One of the two possible origins is that in the 16th century in England, houses had thatched roofs which were one of the few places where animals were able to get warm. When it rained heavily, the

cats and dogs would slide off the roof, making it looked like it was raining cats and dogs.

37. Rub Salt In A Wound, actually was something they used to do to cleanse the wound. Basically, it is to make something that is already difficult, unpleasant, and painful.

38. Red Tape, expressions was because in the past official documents would be covered with red tape. Basically, it means to hinder or prevent action on decision-making. It is usually applied to governments, and other large organizations.

39. Blood Is Thicker Than Water, means that family relationships should be strong. But actually, it is said that soldiers who fought together were blood brothers so to speak.

40. Getting off Scot Free, actually meant you went without paying, as the word Scot was the word used back then for a payment.

41. Barking Up The Wrong Tree, means someone was mistaken in their thought or deed. This expression came about that some hunting dogs would bark up a tree where there was no prey.

42. A Pig In A Poke, meant if you bought a bag with supposedly a pig in it, if you do not look inside it may be something else. We usually mean that we buy something sight unseen.

43. Turn A Blind Eye, is to pretend not to notice. People think that this phrase came about from Horatio Nelson, who used his blind eye to look through his telescope. This way he was able to avoid signals from his superior, who wanted him not to fight. He attacked anyway and won.

44. The expression Scapegoat, came from Leviticus 16: 7-10 where two goats were selected for sacrifice. One was sacrificed, and the other set free.

45. Pride Goes Before A Fall, comes from scripture Proverbs 16:18.

46. Pot Luck, was because if you were invited over for a meal, you may not know what all may be in the stew, soup, or whatever was being served.

47. Pull Out All The Stops. This saying comes from church organs. Pulling out a stop lets air flow through a pipe and then makes the sound. We think this means to go all out to accomplish something.

48. No Rest For The Wicked, came about from the scripture Isaiah 57:21.

49. Break A Leg, means good luck, and is said a lot before someone who is performing. This has a possible weird way of becoming an expression which I will let you look up for yourself.

50. Casting Your Pearls Before, came from the scripture in the Bible Matthew 7:6.

51. Give The Cold Shoulder, is to be unfriendly. It is thought that during medieval times in England, when everyone was done feasting, the host would give his guests a cold piece of meat from the shoulder of beef or pork to show that it was time for everyone to leave. This was strange.

52. Spinning A Yarn, as we call it, was because when people used to spin yarn, they used to tell stories. So basically, it is just telling stories.

53. Riding Shotgun, is to sit in the passenger's seat, which came about during the stagecoach days where someone who sat up front, who was not driving, was holding a shot gun for their protection.

54. Show Your True Colors, meant when a pirate ship would not show the right flag of their ship until it was too late for the other ship to run, and they would overtake them. In our day and time, it meant to reveal one's real nature, which could be that a person who was nice at first, then turned mean or rude.

55. Close But No Cigar, meant close but did not make it. In the 19th century, the adults would win a cigar in games that were playing.

56. Butter Someone Up, is to flatter someone. In India they used to throw balls of butter at their gods to seek favor with them.

57. Put A Sock In It, is to stop talking. Gramophones of the past had no volume control, so that is what they used to bring the sound down

58. Waking Up On The Wrong Side Of The Bed, would mean that you woke up in a bad mood. In the past, it was thought if you got up on the left side of the bed it was the evil side.

59. Get One's Goat, is to find a way to irritate someone. In past times horse racers used to put a goat in the stable with the race horse to calm them down. Competitors would sometimes take the goat out, to make the horse more anxious, and have a better chance for them to win the race.

60. Mad As A Hatter, was called that because hat makers in the earlier centuries used to use mercury in making those hats, which the smell would mentally make them ill. We now use this expression to say that someone was extremely mad.

61. A Spinster, was considered an unmarried woman in her middle age or older.

62. My Ears Are Burning, is that you feel someone is talking about you. People of ancient Rome believed that if your left is burning, it was because someone is planning evil against you, but if it is the right ear, then you are being praised.

63. Every Cloud Has A Silver Lining, is that something negative can have something positive come about from it. The phrase came from the poet John Milton in a poem that he wrote.

64. Rule Of Thumb, came about because craftsmen used to use their thumb for measurements. Basically, it just means using common sense.

65. The Whole Nine Yards, means to do everything you can to accomplish a goal. During World War II they had a nine-yard chain of ammo, and when they used it all at one target, they called it giving the whole nine yards.

66. Pandemonium, which you do not hear that word used much today came from the poem Paradise Lost and the word means **'All The Devils'**. In our day and time, it basically means a chaotic situation.

67. Piece Of Cake, is to accomplish something very easily. It came from a quote from Ogden Nash.

68. Salt Of The Earth, came from the scripture in Matthew 5:13.

69. Take Someone Under Your Wing, and it too is a scripture which came from Luke 12:34.

70. Spill The Beans, means to reveal some information you should not have. This saying came from ancient Greece where they used to vote with black or white

beans, but if someone knocked over the jar, they called it spilling the beans.

71. Eat Humble Pie, is to ask for forgiveness. This kind of pie during middle ages was given to the lower-class people, while all the good meat was given to the upper class.

72. Straight And Narrow, came from the Bible in Matthew 7:14.

73. Let Your Hair Down, meant being inhibited in your behavior. Parisian nobles used to have to wear their hair up, but at the end of the day they would let it down to relax.

74. Hands Down, means without question. This is a horse racing term meaning that the jockey is so far ahead that he can sit back, relax, and still win the race, even without his hands on the reins.

75. Thorn In My Side, is from Bible scripture 2 Corinthians 12:7.

76. Start From Scratch. Racers used to just draw a line in the dirt, as a starting place for a race. To us, it means to start from the beginning.

77. Tongue In Cheek, was a sign of contempt in centuries before.

78. Taken Back, was when a boat stopped moving forward because of a change of direction in the

wind. This usually means that you are taken by surprise.

79. Throw Down The Gauntlet, was part of the suit of armor of the past. When someone threw it to the ground, it met they wanted to have a duel. With us it usually means to confront or challenge someone.

80. Turn Over A New Leaf, was to mean a new start, as to turning the next page, or leaf of a book. In the 16th century, the pages in a book were referred to as leaves. So, tuning over a new leaf meant that one was turning to a blank page

81. Touch And Go, was figured to have come from sailors in shallow water, not knowing the depth of the water. With us it means that the outcome of a situation uncertain.

82. Turn The Other Cheek, was from Bible scripture Luke 6:29.

83. Washing My Hands, of a situation, came about when Pilate washed his hands of being involved in the blood of Jesus. Matthew 27:24 in the Bible. We usually mean that we do not want to get involved anymore, or take the responsibility of an action.

84. Turned The Corner, started out as a sailor's term, as when they went around Cape Horn or the Cape of Good Hope. With us, it means that we have passed the critical point and things start to improve.

85. Wear Your Heart On Your Sleeve, started out when Knights who fought tournaments wore a token on their sleeve from the lady in their life. To us it means exposing our true emotions, and making ourselves vulnerable

86. A Wolf In Sheep's Clothing, came from Bible scripture Matthew 7:15.

I think I will quit right here, as there are thousands upon thousands of old sayings, and expressions, with their meaning that a person could write multiple books on them. If I stirred up your fancy on this, maybe you may want to look up even more, or an expression, or old saying you remember, but not sure when and how it came about.

I would like to wish everybody a **'Great And Glorious Year'**. May this be the year that God takes away the woes of this world, if not, and all this evil progress, then He will finally Rapture His saints before the upcoming **'Great Tribulation'**.

With Love In Christ.

Pastor Lloyd

P.S. For those who are not saved, backslidden, or in doubt of their salvation, it is still not too late. Let me give you two of the sinner's prayers from one of my books that I wrote previously, that you can use, alter, or to even give you an idea of what you may want to say to God.

I

Dear Father in Heaven.

I come to You with a humble heart, asking forgiveness for all of my sins. I know, by Thy word, that I was born, and will die a sinner, but through Jesus Christ only, who died on the cross, and You raised from the dead, bore my sins that I can be saved. I believe You are the true and only living God. I stand firmly, that I believe in the life of Jesus, as told in your Holy Word. I now ask that You wipe my sins away, as if I have never done them. I also ask, for You to send the Holy Spirit to dwell within me. For all this I am eternally grateful. As I send my love up to You my Lord, I ask that You send Your love down upon me, my life, and all that I do. May I be your faithful servant to follow You, lead others to You, and do all that is requested of me, and all that You will guide me to do. In Jesus, most Holy Precious Name I pray.

Amen

II

Dear Precious Heavenly Father.

I come to You in the name of my Lord, and Savior, Jesus Christ,
to ask You to forgive me of all of my sins, cleanse me from all
unrighteousness. I know that my soul is as black as coal, and
that I am a sinner, and have fallen from Your grace and mercy.
Please cleanse me of all my sins and make them white as snow.
I know that Jesus was born of a virgin, and died on a cross, so
a sinner like me might may be saved. Please redeem me from
this wicked, and evil world. Please guide me, in my daily walk.
Let me be a light to others, and understand Thy word, so as I
may lead others to their salvation. I know the time is very, very
short before Jesus comes back at the Rapture, and I have so
much to learn and do. May I always remember to pray to You,
and never forget to thank You for all the blessings You have
bestowed upon me. I know I do not deserve Your forgiveness,
nor by any means have I earned it. By Your grace, and mercy, I
know You have heard my prayers, and all my sins are forgiven,
and that there is a place, even for me, in Heaven. Also, by Your
grace I am forgiven, by Your precious blood, that I have a new
eternal life with You, and by Your love, I know now that I have
an eternal home waiting for me in Heaven. In the name of my
Lord and Savior Jesus Christ.

Amen

What
Christians
Should
Not
Do

On all of the following topics I will just give you one scripture, although there are many more which you can look up on your own.

As Christians we should never quote from false idols like Buddha. The First Commandment of God says:

Exodus 20:3 K.J.V.: Thou shalt have no other gods before Me.

You should not have anything that pertains to any false gods like Buddha, a fertility god, etc.

Exodus 20:4 K.J.V.: Thou shalt not make unto thee any graven image, or any likeness of anything that is in Heaven above, or that is in the earth beneath, or that is in the water under the earth:

As Christians we should not use foul language.

Colossians 3:8 K.J.V.: But now ye also put off all these; anger, wrath, malice, blasphemy, filthy communication out of your mouth.

Do not get involved, or keep any items such as tarot cards, Ouija boards, horoscopes, or anything else that does not pertain to God. I will let you look these up for yourself, as there are so many scriptures in the Bible, that warns you against using these.

Do not seek after those who tell fortunes, or are called mediums, as they are doing the work of the devil.

Leviticus 19:31 N.I.V.: Do not turn to mediums or seek out spiritists, for you will be defiled by them. I am the LORD your God.

What Christians Need

As this evil and wicked world progresses, we as Christians, need to remember and do, two things written in God's Holy Word.

Ephesians 6:11-18 K.J.V.: Put on the whole armor of God, that you may be able to stand against the wiles of the devil. For we wrestle not against flesh and blood, but against principalities, against powers, against the rulers of the darkness of this world, against spiritual wickedness in high places. Wherefore take unto you the whole armour of God, that ye may be able to withstand in the evil day, and having done all, to stand. Stand therefore, having your loins girt about with truth, and having on the breastplate of righteousness; And your feet shod with the preparation of the gospel of peace; Above all, taking the shield of faith, wherewith ye shall be able to quench all the fiery darts of the wicked. And take the helmet of salvation, and the sword of the Spirit, which is the word of God: Praying always with all prayer and supplication in the Spirit, and watching thereunto with all perseverance and supplication for all saints.

Even with all that above, we still need to do the following in the scripture below.

Colossians 3:12-17 K.J.V.: Put on therefore, as the elect of God, holy and beloved, bowels of mercies, kindness, humbleness of mind, meekness, longsuffering; Forbearing one another, and forgiving one another, if any man have a quarrel against any: even as Christ forgave you, so also do ye. And above all these things put on charity, which is the bond of perfectness. And let the peace of God rule in your hearts, to the which also ye are called in one body; and be ye thankful. Let the word of Christ dwell in you richly in all wisdom; teaching and admonishing one another in psalms and hymns and spiritual songs, singing with grace in your hearts to the Lord. And whatsoever ye do in word or deed, do all in the name of the Lord Jesus, giving thanks to God and the Father by Him.

At times of weakness, please remember this.

Isaiah 40:29-31 K.J.V.: He (Talking about God.) giveth power to the faint; and to them that have no might He increaseth strength. Even the youths shall faint and be weary, And the young men shall utterly fall, but they that wait upon the LORD shall renew their strength; they shall mount up with wings as eagles; they shall run, and not be weary; and they shall walk, and not faint.

I said this prayer when writing one of my books, the devil was relentless in his persecution of me, and even tried to take me out, where I was put in the hospital for six days, with among other problems there, my blood pressure was over two hundred. My God over-road him on this, but it was one of the worst times of my life, in which I was going through a deep depression with all that the devil was throwing at me.

Dear Precious, Precious, Heavenly Father.

I come to You in the name of my Lord, and Savior, Jesus Christ. I love You with all my heart, soul, mind, and being, but so many times I fall short of being the Christian I feel You would want me to be. Please help me when I stumble, redirect me when I follow the wrong path, hold me when I am hurting, listen when I need a close friend to talk to, speak to me as I try to listen, give me full understanding when I read **'Thy Holy Scriptures'**, but most of all, know that You are the most important part of my life. Sometimes the words I speak seem so futile, actions, and deeds without merit, words meaningless, and the snares of the evil one surrounds me. Please always guide me, help me, forgive me, love me, especially at times I feel unloved, even though I am not worthy of Your love, or forgiveness. Please watch over me, and never let me far from Thy sight. May I always stay humble in Your presence. My love for You is true, and deep down in my heart. Always, your faithful and loving servant, now and forever.

Amen!

Doubts

In our lives, we have our doubts. Sometimes we use the terminology, **'Lack Of Faith'**. Has this ever happened to saints of the past? Kind David was a prime example, which I will let you look up. He speaks a lot about it in his Psalms.

The one I particularly think about, that I have never heard any Christian or pastor talk about was **'John The Baptist'**. Although he was the prelude to the coming of Jesus, he later had his doubts. First of all, he knew Who Jesus was.

Matthew 3:13-17 K.J.V.: Then cometh Jesus from Galilee to Jordan unto John, to be baptized of him. And John tried to prevent Him, saying, *"I need to be baptized by You, and are You coming to me?"* And Jesus answering said unto him, *"Suffer it to be so now: for thus it becometh us to fulfil all righteousness."* Then he suffered Him. And Jesus, when He was baptized, went up straightway out of the water: and, lo, the Heavens were opened unto Him, and he saw the Spirit of God descending like a dove, and lighting upon Him: And lo a voice from Heaven, saying, *"This is My beloved Son, in Whom I am well pleased."*

Later in life, when John was in prison, his doubts started to waver, so he called his disciples to him, to talk to Jesus with one question.

Matthew 11:2-3 K.J.V.: Now when John had heard in the prison, the works of Christ, he sent two of his disciples, and said unto Him, *"Art thou He that should come, or do we look for another?"*

To let the disciples, know that He is the One, He showed them miracles, and told them what they should relay back to John.

Matthew 11:4 K.J.V.: Jesus answered and said to them, *"Go and tell John the things which you hear and see: The blind see and the lame walk; the lepers are cleansed and the deaf hear; the dead are raised up and the poor have the gospel preached to them. And blessed is he, whosoever shall not be offended in Me."* And as they departed, Jesus began to say unto the multitudes concerning John, *"What went ye out into the wilderness to see? A reed shaken with the wind? But what went ye out for to see? A man clothed in soft raiment? Behold, they that wear soft clothing are in kings' houses. But what did you go out to see? A prophet? Yes, I say to you, and more than a prophet. For this is he, of whom it is written, Behold, I send My messenger before thy face, which shall prepare thy way before thee. Truly I say to you, among those born of women there has not risen one greater than John the Baptist. Yet the least in the Kingdom of the Heavens is greater than he! And from the days of John the Baptist until now the Kingdom of Heaven suffereth violence, and the violent take it by force. For all the prophets and the law prophesied until John."*

I know that was a little lengthy, but I wanted you to know how important John was to the coming of Jesus Christ.

Love

People talk about love with almost anything you can think about. Like, I loved that dinner, surely love that dress, I love my pet, I sure love that book, I loved that movie, and this list can go on and on.

Sometimes people use the word love in talking about a person, who may be a spouse, family member or friend. Sometimes people confuse the word **'Love'** with the word **'Lust'**. I know that I did that a lot earlier in my life, before becoming a Christian with many ladies.

So, what is the best, and purest kind of love. It is the **'Agape'** kind of love. So, what is this kind of love? It is the kind of love that God has for us, and we should have for Him.

1 Corinthians 13:1-3 N.I.V.: If I speak in the tongues of men or of angels, but do not have love, I am only a resounding gong or a clanging cymbal. If I have the gift of prophecy and can fathom all mysteries and all knowledge, and if I have a faith that can move mountains, but do not have love, I am nothing. If I give all I possess to the poor and give over my body to hardship that I may boast, but do not have love, I gain nothing.

So, these scriptures show that the most important thing we can show others is love. Of course, the most important thing we can tell others about is Jesus Christ, and the precious words in the Bible. Does the Bible explain to us in depth about how we should love? Yes.

1st Corinthians 13:4-8 N.I.V.: Love is patient, love is kind. It does not envy, it does not boast, it is not proud. It does not dishonor others, it is not self-seeking, it is not easily angered, it keeps no record of wrongs. Love does not delight in evil but rejoices with the truth. It always protects, always trusts, always hopes, always perseveres. Love never fails. But where there are prophecies, they will cease; where there are tongues, they will be stilled; where there is knowledge, it will pass away.

You really need to read the last scriptures, and then truly understand about the love that God wants us to show to others.

My Special Prayer, For Those Who Read This Book.

May God love you and keep you,
and help make your life grand.
May He give you the wisdom,
from the Bible and my books to understand.
I pray He helps you and guides you,
on paths that are not straight.
That He gives you patience each day,
when your answer to prayers you must wait.
May your family be saved,
or will be before it's too late.
So together you'll be in Heaven,
with all He did create.
I pray all your blessings come,
from the Lord up above.
And that you receive it with gladness,
and it reminds you of God's love.
I also pray that God,
fills all of your needs.
And some of your wants too,
if they are not wanted through greed.
So, I want to thank God that He heard me,
and gives you His very best.

In whatever He does in your life,

that you know with Him you are blessed.

Lastly, I say that I love you,

till in Heaven we shall meet.

As we all bow down together,

at **'God's Holy Feet'**.

Amen

'So Be It'

'With Agape Love. From My Heart!'

Pastor Lloyd E. Stinnett D. D.

I have written some children's books. One is out now called: **'Ruffles The Dragon.'** Watch out for episode II called: **'Ruffles' Scuffle.'** Also, I have the first book of six episodes out called: **'A Flea, A Fly, And A Mouse.'** Also, coming out soon is a Christmas book called: **'Twas' The First Night Of Christmas',** and a children's/puppet play book called: **'The Witness.'**

And for the adults I have a few books out. Three Christian books called: **'Many Things Most Christians Do Not Know,' 'A Must Read For Everyone,'** and **'Live Life, Laughter, And Love.'** I also wrote a poetry book called: **'Laughter, Inspiration, Spiritual, And Tears.'** Also coming out this year will be a book called: **'It's So Funny.'**

These books can be bought at Amazon, Barnes And Noble, and 25,000-30,000 retailers around the world.

'With Love In Christ, And Stay Safe.'
Pastor Lloyd E. Stinnett D. D.

Printed in the United States
by Baker & Taylor Publisher Services